Keyboard
Rock Songbook

INTRODUCTION

Welcome to FastTrack™!

Hope you are ready to play some hits. Have you and your friends formed a band? Or do you feel like soloing with the CD? Either way, make sure you're relaxed and comfortable... it's time to play!

As always, don't try to bite off more than you can chew. If your hands hurt, take some time off. If you get frustrated, turn off your keyboard, sit back and just listen to the CD. If you forget a technique, rhythm, or note position, go back and learn it. If you're doing fine, think about finding an agent.

CONTENTS

ABOUT THE CD

Each song in the book is included on the CD, so you can hear how it sounds and play along when you're ready.

Each example on the CD is preceded by one measure of "clicks" to indicate the tempo and meter. Pan right to hear the keyboard part emphasized. Pan left to hear the accompaniment emphasized.

ISBN 978-1-4234-9572-7

HAL•LEONARD®
CORPORATION
7777 W. BLUEMOUND RD. P.O. BOX 13819 MILWAUKEE, WI 53213

Visit Hal Leonard Online at
www.halleonard.com

LEARN SOMETHING NEW EACH DAY

We know you're eager to play, but first we need to explain a few new things. We'll make it brief—only one page...

Melody and Lyrics

The additional musical staff on top shows you the song's melody and lyrics. This way, you can follow along more easily as you play your accompaniment part, whether it's chords or harmony or a blazing solo.

And if you happen to be playing with a singer, this staff is their part.

Endings

1st and 2nd Endings

These are indicated by brackets and numbers:

Simply play the song through to the first ending, then repeat back to the first repeat sign, or beginning of the song (whichever is the case). Play through the song again, but skip the first ending and play the second ending.

D.S. al Coda

When you see these words, go back and repeat from this symbol: 𝄋

Play until you see the words "To Coda" then skip to the Coda, indicated by this symbol: 𝄌

Now just finish the song.

That's about it! Enjoy the music...

Are You Gonna Be My Girl

Words and Music by Cameron Muncey and Nicholas Cester

Intro
Fast Rock ♩ = 206

*Go! _____

* Sing 1st time only.

Play one octave lower throughout

1. So,
2. Well, it's a   one, two, three, take my

hand and come with me be-cause you look so fine and I real-ly want to make you mine.

A

N.C.

I say you look so fine and I real-ly want to make you mine.

A

N.C.

Well, four, five, six, come on ___

___ and get your kicks. Now you don't need mon-ey { when you look like that, do you, hon-ey? / with a face like that, do ya? ___ }

A

N.C.

Pre-Chorus

Big ___ black boots, long ___ brown hair.

She's ___ so sweet with ___ her get ___ back stare.

Chorus

Well, I could see ___ you home with me, ___ but you were with ___ ___ an-oth-er man, ___ yeah. ___ I ___ know

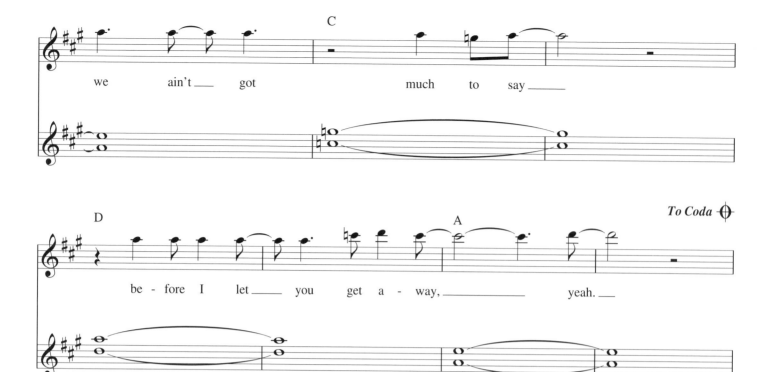

we ain't ___ got   much   to   say ___

To Coda ⊕

be - fore I   let ___ you   get a - way, _____   yeah. __

I   said,

"Are   you   gon - na   be   my   girl?" __

I   said, "Are   you   gon - na   be   my   girl?" _

Interlude

D.S. al Coda

Ah. _____

Coda

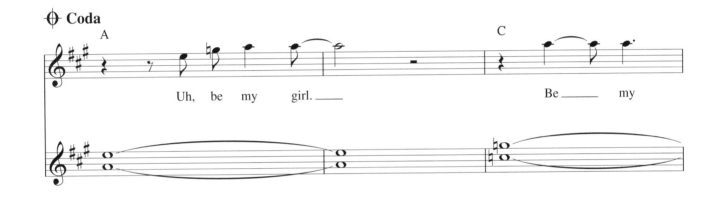

Uh, be my girl. _____ Be _____ my

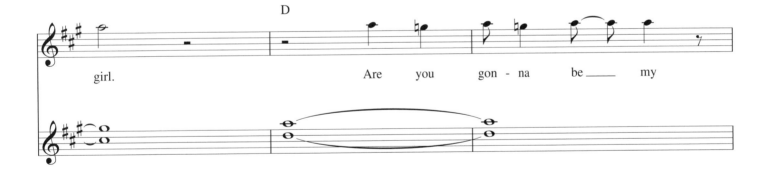

girl. Are you gon - na be _____ my

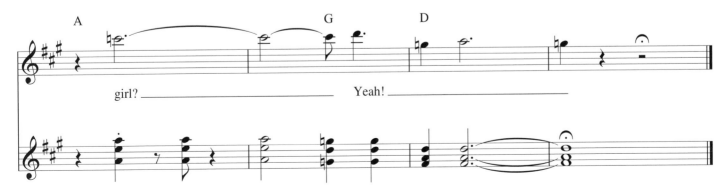

girl? _____ Yeah! _____

② Clocks

Words and Music by Guy Berryman, Jon Buckland, Will Champion and Chris Martin

things un-said. ___ Shoot an ap - ple off my head. ___ And a
on my seas, ___ curse missed op - por - tu - ni - ties. ___ Am I

trou - ble that can't be named. ___ A tig - er's wait - ing
a part ___ of the cure ___ or am I part of

Chorus

to be tamed. ___ }
the dis - ease? ___ } Sing - in': You ___

___ are. ___ You ___

To Coda

are. ___

Interlude

Coda

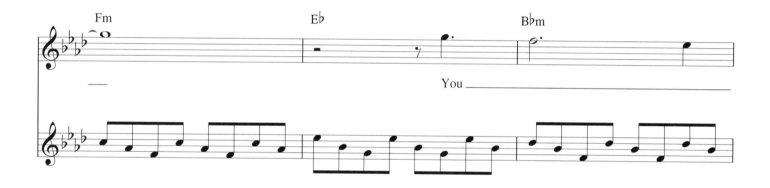

Bridge

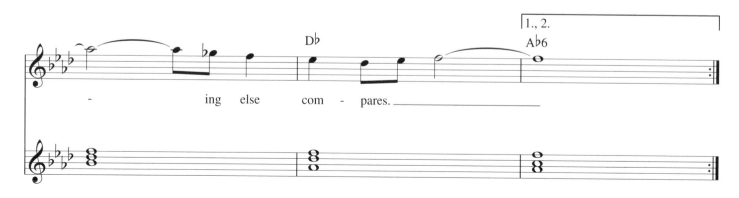

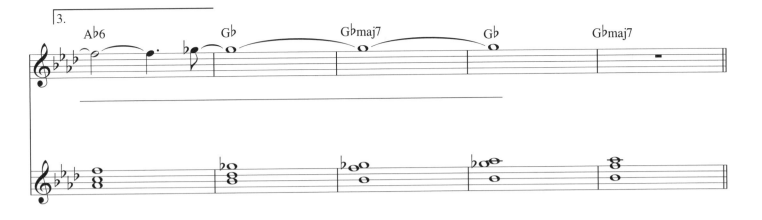

Breakdown

Interlude

Outro

Home,   home, ___   where I want - ed ___ to   go.

Dani California

Words and Music by Anthony Kiedis, Flea, John Frusciante and Chad Smith

Play one octave lower throughout

1.

what in the world does your com - pa - ny take ____ me for?

2.

just an - oth - er way to sur - vive. ____
it ____ on - ly hurts when I laugh. ____

Cal - i - for -

Chorus

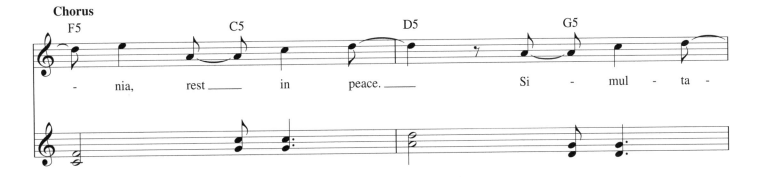

- nia, rest ____ in peace. ____ Si - mul - ta -

- ne - ous ____ re - lease. ____ Cal - i - for - nia, show ___ your teeth, ___

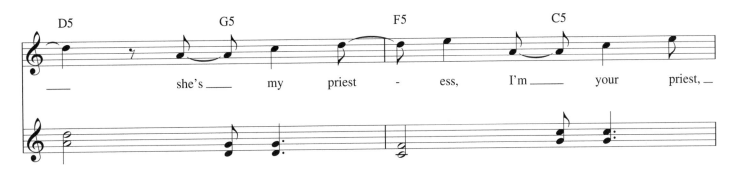

____ she's ____ my priest - ess, I'm _____ your priest, ___

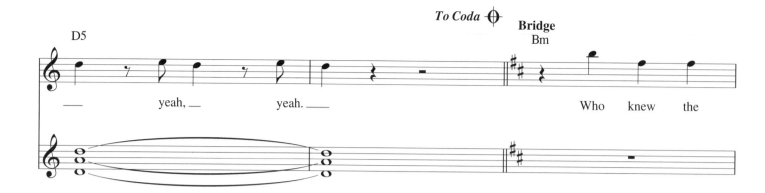

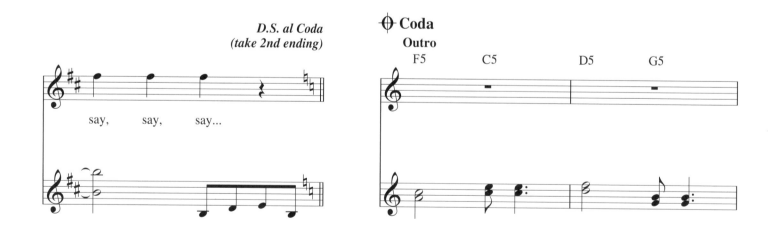

Grenade

**Words and Music by Bruno Mars, Ari Levine, Philip Lawrence,
Christopher Steven Brown, Claude Kelly and Andrew Wyatt**

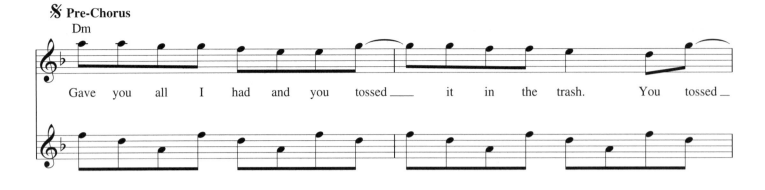

𝄋 Pre-Chorus

Gave you all I had and you tossed ___ it in the trash. You tossed ___

___ it in the trash; you did. ___ To give ___ me all your love is all ___

___ I ev - er asked, 'cause ___ what you don't un - der - stand ___ is, I'd catch a gre - nade ___

𝄋 𝄋 Chorus

___ for ya, ___ throw my hand on a blade ___ for ya. ___

I'd jump in front of a train ___ for ya. ___ You know I'd do an - y - thing ___

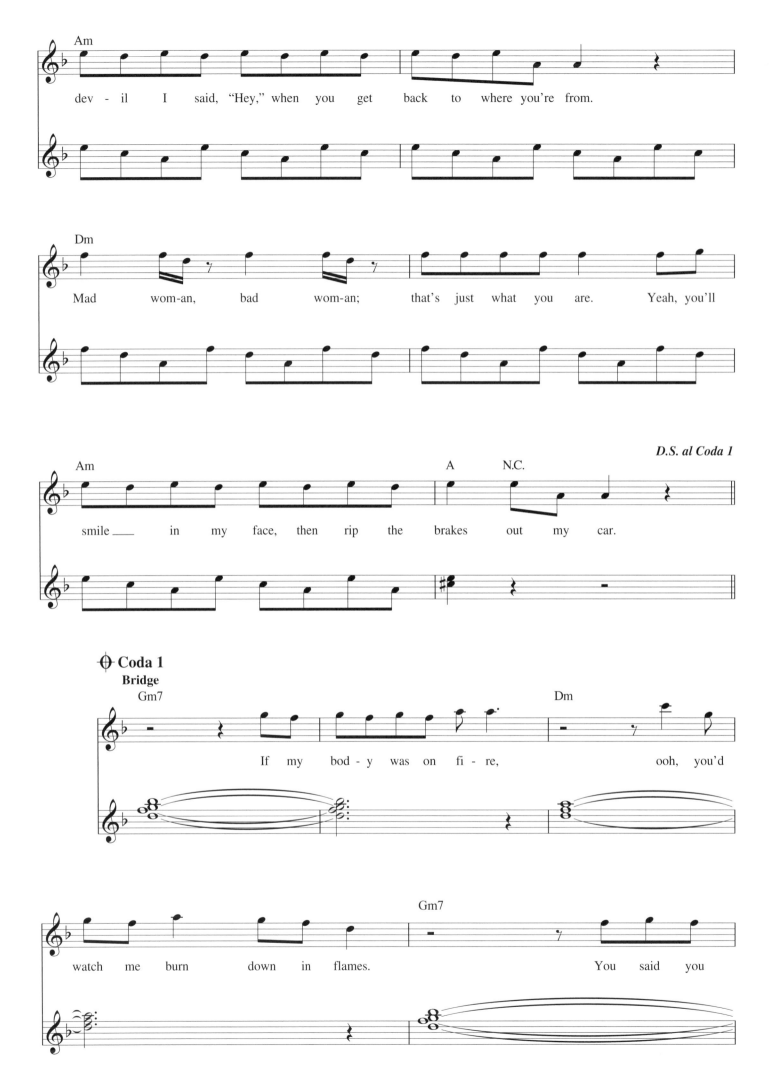

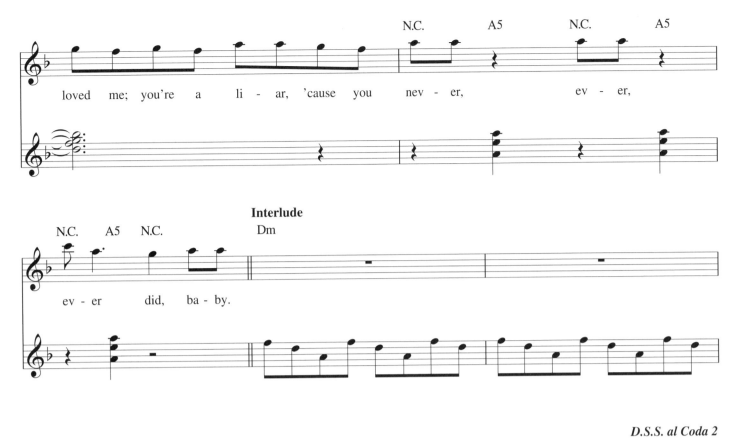

loved me; you're a li - ar, 'cause you nev - er, ev - er,

Interlude

ev - er did, ba - by.

D.S.S. al Coda 2

But dar - ling, I'd still catch a gre - nade

Coda 2
Outro

{ No, you won't }
{ You nev - er } do the same.

1.
You would - n't do the same.
2.
No, no, no.

◆4 Gives You Hell

Words and Music by Tyson Ritter and Nick Wheeler

Intro
Moderately ♩ = 100

Fender Rhodes sound
Play one octave lower throughout

Verse

1. I wake up ev - 'ry eve - ning
where's your pick - et fence, _ love,

with a big smile on my face, and it nev - er feels out of place. _
and where's that shin - y car, and did it ev - er get you far? _

And you're still prob - 'ly work - ing
You nev - er seemed _ so tense, _ love.

D.S.S. al Coda 2

Home

Words and Music by Chris Daughtry

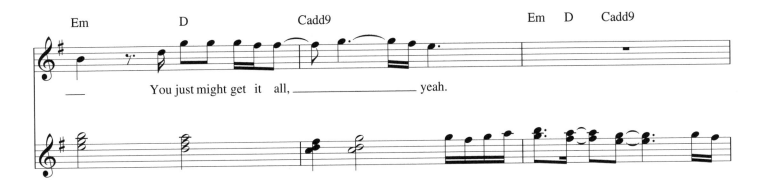

You just might get it all, _____ yeah.

D.S. al Coda

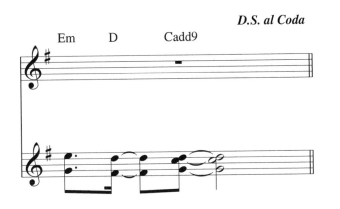

⊕ **Coda**

old. _   I said, these

plac - es   and __   these fac - es   are get - ting   old, ___   so I'm go - in' home. _

I'm go - in' home. _

Additional Lyrics

2. The miles are getting longer, it seems,
   The closer I get to you.
   I've not always been the best man or friend for you,
   But your love remains true.
   And I don't know why
   You always seem to give me another try.

🌑 21 Guns

Words and Music by David Bowie, John Phillips, Billie Joe Armstrong, Mike Pritchard and Frank Wright

- contains samples of "All The Young Dudes" by David Bowie and "San Francisco (Be Sure To Wear Some Flowers In Your Hair)" by John Phillip

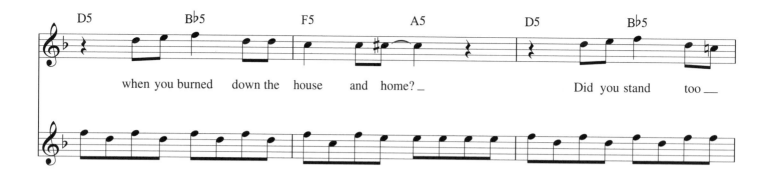

when you burned down the house and home? _ Did you stand too _

close to the fire _ like a li - ar look-ing for for-give - ness from a stone? _

Guitar Solo

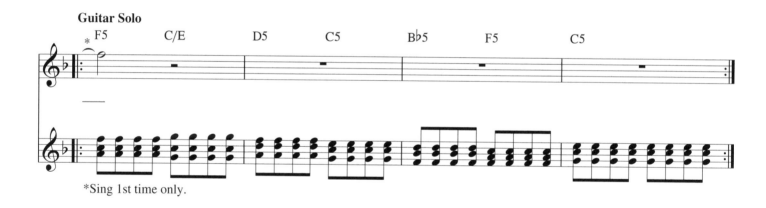

*Sing 1st time only.

Interlude

Verse

3. When it's time _ to _ live and let die _ and you can't _ get an -

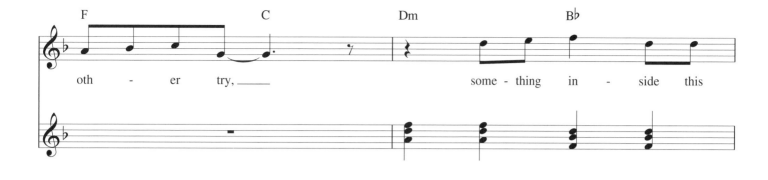

oth - er try, _____ some - thing in - side this

D.S. al Coda

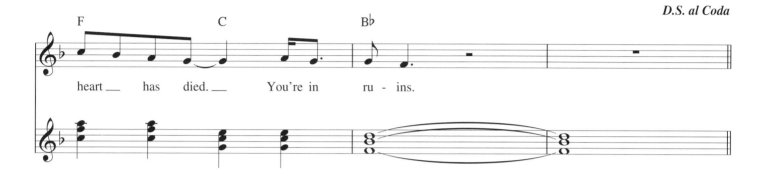

heart __ has died. __ You're in ru - ins.

⊕ Coda

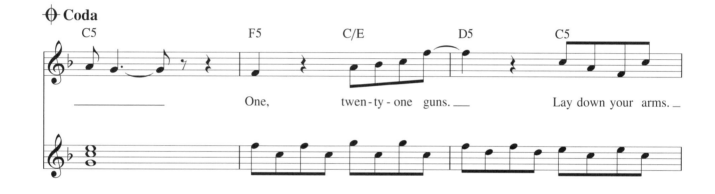

_____ One, twen-ty-one guns. __ Lay down your arms. _

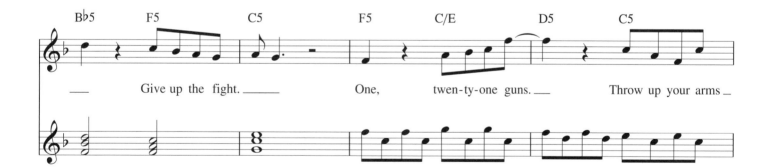

__ Give up the fight. _____ One, twen-ty-one guns. __ Throw up your arms _

__ in - to the sky, _____ you and I. _____

Use Somebody

Words and Music by Caleb Followill, Nathan Followill, Jared Followill and Matthew Followill

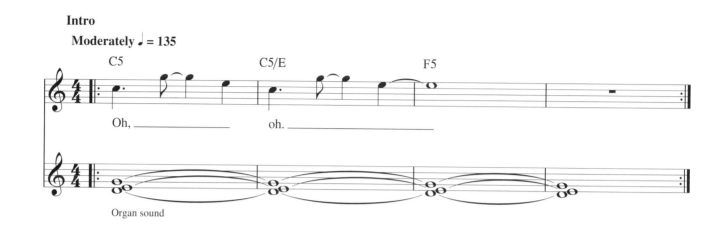

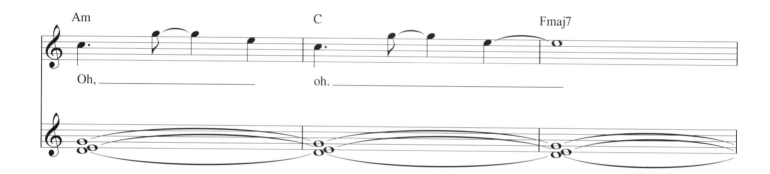

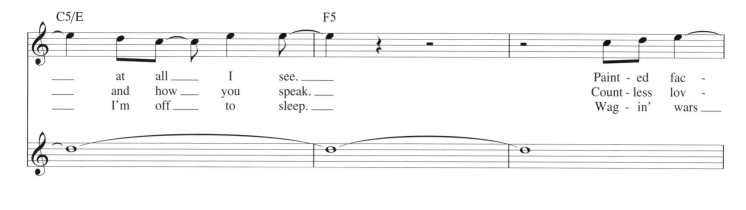

at all ___ I see. ___
and how ___ you speak. ___
I'm off ___ to sleep. ___

Paint - ed fac -
Count - less lov -
Wag - in' wars ___

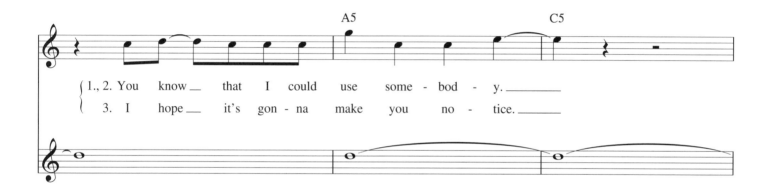

- es fill ___ the plac - es I ___ can't reach. ___
- ers un - der cov - er of ___ the street. ___
to shake ___ the po - et and ___ the beat. ___

1., 2. You know ___ that I could use some - bod - y. ___
3. I hope ___ it's gon - na make you no - tice. ___

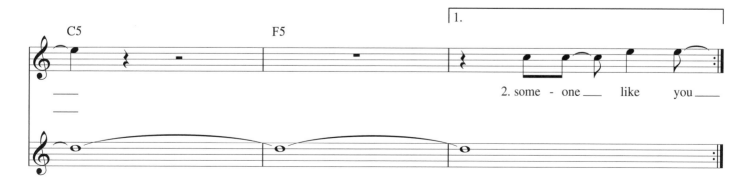

You know ___ that I could use some - bod - y, ___
I hope ___ it's gon - na make you no - tice ___

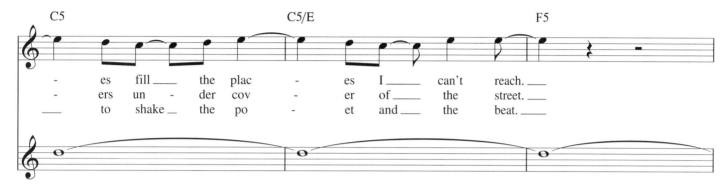

1.

___
___

2. some - one ___ like you ___

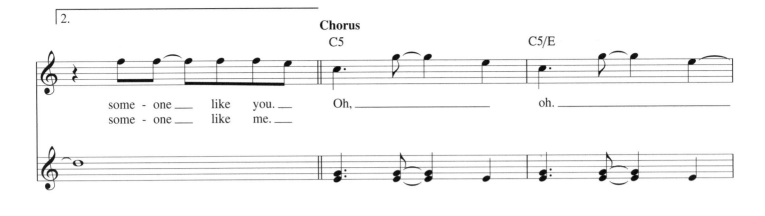

some - one ___ like you. ___ Oh, _____ oh. _____
some - one ___ like me. ___

2. Some - one ___ like me. ___ Oh, _____

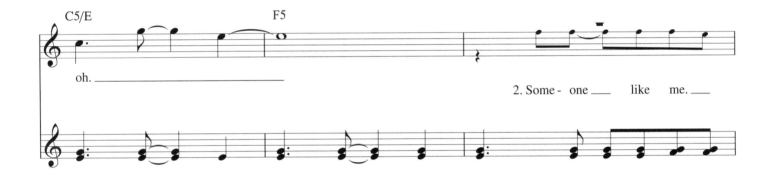

oh. _____ 2. Some - one ___ like me. ___

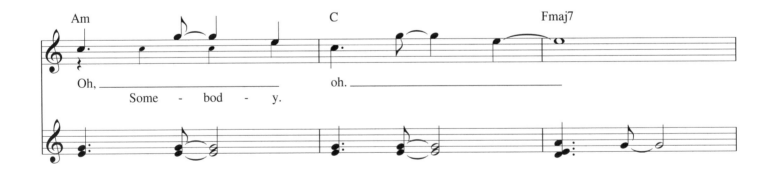

Oh, _____ oh. _____
Some - bod - y.

Oh, _____ oh. _____

Oh, _____ oh. _____ Some - one _ like you, _

Chorus

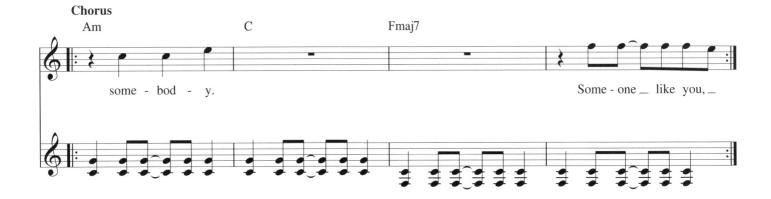

some - bod - y. Some - one _ like you, _

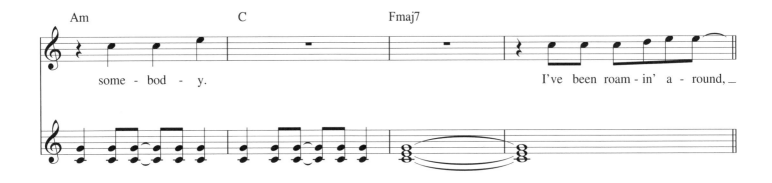

some - bod - y. I've been roam - in' a - round, _

Outro

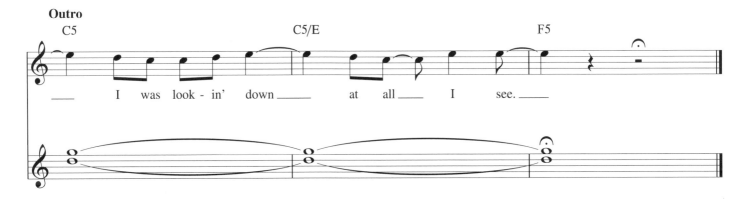

_ I was look - in' down _ at all _ I see. _

FastTrack is the fastest way for beginners to learn to play the instrument they just bought. **FastTrack** is different from other method books: we've made our book/CD packs user-friendly with plenty of cool songs that make it easy and fun for players to teach themselves. Plus, the last section of the **FastTrack** books have the same songs so that students can form a band and jam together. Songbooks for Guitar, Bass, Keyboard and Drums are all compatible, and feature eight songs including hits such as Wild Thing • Twist and Shout • Layla • Born to Be Wild • and more! All packs include a great play-along CD with a professional-sounding back-up band.

FASTTRACK GUITAR

For Electric or Acoustic Guitar – or both!
by Blake Neely & Jeff Schroedl
Book/CD Packs

Teaches music notation, tablature, full chords and power chords, riffs, licks, scales, and rock and blues styles. Method Book 1 includes 73 songs and examples.

LEVEL 1

00697282	Method Book – 9" x 12"	$7.99
00695390	Method Book – 5½" x 5"	$7.95
00697287	Songbook 1 – 9" x 12"	$12.95
00695397	Songbook 1 – 5½" x 5"	$9.95
00695343	Songbook 2	$12.95
00696438	Rock Songbook 1	$12.99
00696057	DVD	$7.99

LEVEL 2

00697286	Method Book	$9.99
00697296	Songbook 1	$12.95
00695344	Songbook 2	$12.95

CHORDS & SCALES

00697291	9" x 12"	$9.95
00696588	Spanish Edition	$9.99

FASTTRACK BASS

by Blake Neely & Jeff Schroedl
Book/CD Packs

Everything you need to know about playing the bass, including music notation, tablature, riffs, licks, scales, syncopation, and rock and blues styles. Method Book 1 includes 75 songs and examples.

LEVEL 1

00697284	Method Book – 9" x 12"	$7.95
00697289	Songbook 1 – 9" x 12"	$12.95
00695400	Songbook 1 – 5½" x 5"	$9.95
00695368	Songbook 2	$12.95
00696440	Rock Songbook 1	$12.99
00696058	DVD	$7.99

LEVEL 2

00697294	Method Book	$9.95
00697298	Songbook 1	$12.95
00695369	Songbook 2	$12.95

FASTTRACK KEYBOARD

For Electric Keyboard, Synthesizer, or Piano
by Blake Neely & Gary Meisner
Book/CD Packs

Learn how to play that piano today! With this book you'll learn music notation, chords, riffs, licks, scales, syncopation, and rock and blues styles. Method Book 1 includes over 87 songs and examples.

LEVEL 1

00697283	Method Book – 9" x 12"	$7.99
00697288	Songbook 1 – 9" x 12"	$12.95
00695366	Songbook 2	$12.95
00696439	Rock Songbook 1	$12.99
00696060	DVD	$7.99

LEVEL 2

00697293	Method Book	$9.95
00697297	Songbook 1	$12.95
00695370	Songbook 2	$12.99

CHORDS & SCALES

00697292	9" x 12"	$9.95

FASTTRACK DRUM

by Blake Neely & Rick Mattingly
Book/CD Packs

With this book, you'll learn music notation, riffs and licks, syncopation, rock, blues and funk styles, and improvisation. Method Book 1 includes over 75 songs and examples.

LEVEL 1

00697285	Method Book – 9" x 12"	$7.95
00695396	Method Book – 5½" x 5"	$7.95
00697290	Songbook 1 – 9" x 12"	$12.95
00695367	Songbook 2	$12.95
00696441	Rock Songbook 1	$12.99

LEVEL 2

00697295	Method Book	$9.95
00697299	Songbook 1	$12.95
00695371	Songbook 2	$12.95
00696059	DVD	$7.99

FASTTRACK SAXOPHONE

by Blake Neely
Book/CD Packs

With this book, you'll learn music notation; riffs, scales, keys; syncopation; rock and blues styles; and more. Includes 72 songs and examples.

LEVEL 1

00695241	Method Book	$7.95
00695409	Songbook	$12.95

FASTTRACK HARMONICA

by Blake Neely & Doug Downing
Book/CD Packs

These books cover all you need to learn C Diatonic harmonica, including: music notation • singles notes and chords • riffs, licks & scales • syncopation • rock and blues styles. Method Book 1 includes over 70 songs and examples.

LEVEL 1

00695407	Method Book	$7.99
00695574	Songbook	$12.95

LEVEL 2

00695889	Method Book	$9.95

FASTTRACK LEAD SINGER

by Blake Neely
Book/CD Packs

Everything you need to be a great singer, including: how to read music, microphone tips, warm-up exercises, ear training, syncopation, and more. Method Book 1 includes 80 songs and examples.

LEVEL 1

00695408	Method Book	$7.99
00695410	Songbook	$12.95
00696589	Spanish Edition	$7.99

LEVEL 2

00695892	Songbook 1	$12.95

FOR MORE INFORMATION, SEE YOUR LOCAL MUSIC DEALER,
OR WRITE TO:

HAL•LEONARD® CORPORATION

7777 W. BLUEMOUND RD. P.O. BOX 13819 MILWAUKEE, WI 53213

Visit Hal Leonard online at **www.halleonard.com**

Prices, contents, and availability subject to change without notice. Some products may not be available outside the U.S.A.

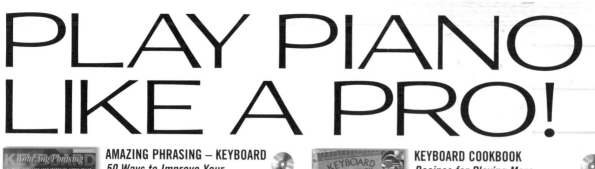

PLAY PIANO LIKE A PRO!

AMAZING PHRASING – KEYBOARD
50 Ways to Improve Your Improvisational Skills
by Debbie Denke

Amazing Phrasing is for any keyboard player interested in learning how to improvise and how to improve their creative phrasing. This method is divided into three parts: melody, harmony, and rhythm & style. The companion CD contains 44 full-band demos for listening, as well as many play-along examples so you can practice improvising over various musical styles and progressions.
00842030 Book/CD Pack $16.95

BEBOP LICKS FOR PIANO
A Dictionary of Melodic Ideas for Improvisation
by Les Wise

Written for the musician who is interested in acquiring a firm foundation for playing jazz, this unique book/CD pack presents over 800 licks. By building up a vocabulary of these licks, players can connect them together in endless possibilities to form larger phrases and complete solos. The book includes piano notation, and the CD contains helpful note-for-note demos of every lick.
00311854 Book/CD Pack $16.99

BOOGIE WOOGIE FOR BEGINNERS
by Frank Paparelli

A short easy method for learning to play boogie woogie, designed for the beginner and average pianist. Includes: exercises for developing left-hand bass • 25 popular boogie woogie bass patterns • arrangements of "Down the Road a Piece" and "Answer to the Prayer" by well-known pianists • a glossary of musical terms for dynamics, tempo and style.
00120517 .... $7.95

INTROS, ENDINGS & TURNAROUNDS FOR KEYBOARD
Essential Phrases for Swing, Latin, Jazz Waltz, and Blues Styles
by John Valerio

Learn the intros, endings and turnarounds that all of the pros know and use! This new keyboard instruction book by John Valerio covers swing styles, ballads, Latin tunes, jazz waltzes, blues, major and minor keys, vamps and pedal tones, and more.
00290525 .... $12.95

JAZZ PIANO VOICINGS
An Essential Resource for Aspiring Jazz Musicians
by Rob Mullins

The jazz idiom can often appear mysterious and difficult for musicians who were trained to play other types of music. Long-time performer and educator Rob Mullins helps players enter the jazz world by providing voicings that will help the player develop skills in the jazz genre and start sounding professional right away – without years of study! Includes a "Numeric Voicing Chart," chord indexes in all 12 keys, info about what range of the instrument you can play chords in, and a beginning approach to bass lines.
00310914 .... $19.95

KEYBOARD COOKBOOK
Recipes for Playing More Than 40 Styles

Spice up your playing today! This book provides the essential ingredients for 40 popular piano styles, including: Bebop • Bluegrass • Classic Rock • Classical • Contemporary R&B • Cool Jazz • Delta Blues • Early Rock 'n' Roll • Folk • Motown • New Age • Ragtime • Soul • Stride • Tango • and more. The CD includes demonstration tracks for all 40 styles, so you'll have a recipe for success!
00311009 Book/CD Pack $18.95

101 KEYBOARD TIPS
Stuff All the Pros Know and Use
by Craig Weldon

Ready to take your keyboard playing to the next level? This book will show you how. *101 Keyboard Tips* presents valuable how-to insight that players of all styles and levels can benefit from. The text, photos, music, diagrams and accompanying CD provide an essential, easy-to-use resource for a variety of topics, including: techniques, improvising and soloing, equipment, practicing, ear training, performance, theory, and much more.
00310933 Book/CD Pack $14.95

OSCAR PETERSON – JAZZ EXERCISES, MINUETS, ETUDES & PIECES FOR PIANO

Legendary jazz pianist Oscar Peterson has long been devoted to the education of piano students. In this book he offers dozens of pieces designed to empower the student, whether novice or classically trained, with the technique needed to become an accomplished jazz pianist.
00311225 .... $12.99

PIANO FITNESS
A Complete Workout
by Mark Harrison

This book will give you a thorough technical workout, while having fun at the same time! The accompanying CD allows you to play along with a rhythm section as you practice your scales, arpeggios, and chords in all keys. Instead of avoiding technique exercises because they seem too tedious or difficult, you'll look forward to playing them. Various voicings and rhythmic settings, which are extremely useful in a variety of pop and jazz styles, are also introduced.
00311995 Book/CD Pack $19.99

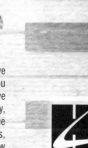

THE TOTAL KEYBOARD PLAYER
A Complete Guide to the Sounds, Styles & Sonic Spectrum
by Dave Adler

Do you play the keyboards in your sleep? Do you live for the feel of the keys beneath your fingers? If you answered in the affirmative, then read on, brave musical warrior! All you seek is here: the history, the tricks, the stops, the patches, the plays, the holds, the fingering, the dynamics, the exercises, the magic. Everything you always wanted to know about keyboards, all in one amazing key-centric compendium.
00311977 Book/CD Pack $19.99

Prices, contents, and availability subject to change without notice.

HAL•LEONARD®
7777 W. BLUEMOUND RD. P.O. BOX 13819
MILWAUKEE, WISCONSIN 53213

www.halleonard.com

0811